TANNER
AND THE WOOD OF SHADOWS

Claudia J. Schulze / Tim Holden
Anke Hartmann

© Claudia J. Schulze
Herstellung und Verlag: BOD- Books-on Demand, Norderstedt
ISBN: 978-3-7448-3840-5

Tanner was almost 10 years old. He had brown hair and blue eyes.

Actually, he was like most kids at his age except perhaps that he always seemed to be surrounded by animals.

It had started almost as soon as he could walk.

Beginning at a very early age, he was always in the forest watching the animals. Not even the shy animals, like the deer, ran away when Tanner appeared.

Sometimes they stood right in front of him and looked at him calmly.

They were beautiful and so majestic that they almost took Tanner's breath away.

These moments were very special to him.

Although they were so powerful with their antlers and hooves, Tanner never ever felt threatened by them. When he looked into the deers' dark eyes he felt protected - as if no one could possibly harm him. In the forest Tanner felt the safest.

He loved everything that he could see and experience there.

It wasn't only what he could see, however.

You could take in the forest with all of the senses. It could be smelled, heard, felt and even tasted.

The forest was transformed into something new as the seasons changed. Tanner found this exciting as well. There was nothing in the forest that didn't excite him. In the forest there was nothing that could not have possibly happened. The entire forest with all of its animals appeared to him as one great miracle composed of many small ones - whether it was Roy, the tame rabbit, with the short ears, or Horst, the curious boar. Life was everywhere. Especially in the summer, everything there shimmered, sparkled and rustled through the trees in the most miraculous way.
When the boar raced through the underbrush they make quite a rumble, but the deer could hardly be heard.

All of the variety and all of the nuances that he found contained in the small realm of his beloved forest fascinated him. Most of all, he had literally lived in that forest.

Indeed if it weren't for his mother, he would have lived in the forest.

At one time he had a sister and a father, but they were no longer there.

Tanner hardly spoke about it, but the fact was that he was the only one left for his mother now. Therefore Tanner had abandoned his plan to live in the woods. Actually it was much more pleasant to live in a house - especially at night and during the winter.

Of course he couldn't imagine life without his mother, and he also had a cat that lived exclusively in the house.

Tanner would have to do without his cat, too, if he chose to live in the forest, so he stayed home instead. And so he had just stayed home. But that took none of the forest's magic.

He loved how the squirrels jumped from tree to tree. He wished that he could do that. They appeared to fly as the color of their fur warmed the forest for a brief moment. While hiding their nuts for the winter they paid no attention to whether or not Tanner was actually watching them.

They must have known that they could trust him. Tanner would never have done anything to harm an animal in the forest. It would have been unthinkable.

Such a thing was unthinkable. He couldn't even begin to say what he liked most in the woods, for there were so many things. He liked the otters and he admired the elegance of the owls as they glided silently through the night sky.
There was an owl named Gerda. Tanner could have sworn that she made her evening flights around his house especially artful because she secretly knew that Tanner was watching.
He watched every night. Tanner was lucky to live so close to the forest that he could watch some of the animals from his window.
Nothing calmed him better after a hard day than his evening hours spent by the window.
Sometimes they came up very close to his house and slept near him.
Not many children could say that.
After a difficult day nothing would calm him better down than his nocturnal hours at the window when he looked at the animals.

There was something else that made Tanner different. Something that he wished he could change. Tanner found interacting with other people difficult- especially with adults. They were as unpredictable as they were large. He felt smothered by their size as well as their piercing looks and seemingly insatiable talka- tiveness. They were everywhere.

Tanner avoided them whenever he could and was quite creative in doing so. Especially when they spoke in an unfriendly way to their animals like the lumberjack that Tanner sometimes saw with his dog. Once he even saw him try and kick his dog. Fortunately he missed, but Tanner promised himself that he would take action against this man someday. He just didn't know what that might be. Fortunately he had not hit him, but Tanner had promised to himself to someday do something against this man. He just did not know what that might be and he was still looking for an idea. However although the woodman´s dog looked quite dangerous at first glance, Tanner didn´t feel the slightest fear, for the dog´s body language pointed to a friendly animal and supported his impression of the dog. He was afraid of the lumberjack.

With people it was very different than with animals. In fact it was completely different, and that is why Tanner wanted to be a veterinarian someday.

The animals seemed to know this already. How else can it be explained that, whenever one was sick, it would come to him in whatever form it could - flying, fluttering, or walking.

Birds with broken wings, orphaned chicks, cats with wounded paws, or a dog that had escaped his master.

Once there was also an owl with a wounded beak, a small wild pig, and a mole that had been injured by a fallen brick.

Each had come to Tanner in its own way, and he had been able to help them all.

He wished for nothing more than to be able to help them. Now and then, however, he thought how wonderful it could be if he could help himself and become less afraid of other people. But that was only a fleeting thought.

Although he always found a good and quick solution when it came to healing a bird's wing, saving a butterfly or feedling a young bird with a pipette, he couldn't figure out a way to help himself. To him, it was a complete mystery how he could possibly do something similar for himself although it was absolutely necessary.

To be honest: it would have been absolutely necessary. In school, he could hardly produce a reasonable sentence, he allowed himself to be pushed aside at the baker's, and the school bus driver was his worst problem. Tanner started to tremble whenever he had to show him his ticket. As soon as an adult looked at him, he was unable to utter a word.

Some of the kids in school even started making fun of him because of it.

Especially Kai, the star of the football-team.

But Tanner couldn't help it. Whenever he saw the bus driver, he felt bad.

He had already stopped believing that this could ever change. But that was before that day he met a mysterious hedgehog. Tanner had heard a noise.

He had discovered the hedgehog in the piles of leaves on the ground and he just wanted to go back into the house to get an egg from the fridge for him. But before he could move, the hedgehog began to hiss. He hissed clearly.

Tanner was a little startled. So he leaned toward the hedgehog down to see if he was sick or if he was hurt.

His face was now directly in front of the head of the hedgehog. He noticed with relief that his eyes were completely clear, not cloudy like a sick animal's eye would be.

"Hello Sting" he said softly to the hedgehog.

He found that this name would fit. Tanner tilted his head slightly to hear whether the hedgehog was breathing evenly. Out of a sudden he felt something wet nudge in his ear. The hedgehog had nudged him with his tiny, wet hedgehog nose into the middle of his right ear.

Then he turned and disappeared with his crooked little legs back into the night. Tanner stared into the night, trying to see Sting again but the hedgehog was gone.

On the floor he found a raven's feather in between some autumn leaves through which the hedgehog had made its way into the night. Tanner stared at the ground after Sting had disappeared and took at least the feather with him, right into his room. Above the bed he found a good place for it. He could not fall asleep because he was thinking about Sting, but when the moon reached the window and the soft moon painted a mellow, feathery shadow onto the wall, he out of a sudden, felt that finally he was tired.

After Tanner had finally fallen asleep, he dreamed of Sting, who ran through a summer meadow, with only the trembling of grass whispering to Tanner where Sting was - moving along very quietly.

In his dream Sting went a long way. Finding a way through all the seasons and through each spot, the forest had possibly to offer.

Tanner could hardly sleep because he had to think of Sting.

All the next morning he still thought of the hedgehog as he boarded the school- bus.

Not even the bird on the tree opposite the bus stop could tear him from his thoughts.

The bus driver was, while driving, scary as ever, gazing stolidly at Tanner. Tanner suddenly felt bad, as always when he saw the bus driver.

But today was a little different than usual, although it first seemed exactly as it always used to be. But all of a sudden there was a

strange sound. It was the croak of a frog and it seemed to come out of the mouth of

the bus driver although the driver kept his lips pressed together tightly.

The sound was so funny and so perfectly combined with the face of the bus driver that Tanner had to grin.

Suddenly he felt no fear any more. Perfectly calm, he showed the frog - bus driver his ticket. Then he sat down – completely without feeling weakness in his knees - to his seat.

Yet he did not come to consider, that the hedgehog could have had anything to do with it. Only while school went on, he started believing that the hedgehog had mesmerized him with his little nose.

The English teacher suddenly sounded like a shaggy, affectionate old cat. The gym teacher, however, sounded like a very tough, but slightly weak donkey and the baker was wrapped up in the choppy cooing of a warm-hearted pigeon.

All of a sudden Tanner understood, that the sounds should show him who these people were if they were animals. He understood that he needed to have no fear of them anymore because like that they weren't unpredictable giants any more. On his way home his fear at once, however, was back. The noise that surrounded the woodman he saw was the noise of a big swarm of irritated wasps.

Suddenly Tanner realized what a great gift the little hedgehog had given to him. He had given to him the skill to judge by the help of his ears, when it was worth being afraid and when it was not worth it at all.

Tanner thought that the hedgehog would have been afraid of the forest worker as well. For sure he also would have run away. And therefore Tanner regarded it no longer as a kind of shame, since he also did exactly that. He ran as fast as he could.

At home he told Mom, who was playing with the cat, of Sting, the hedgehog and the forest worker who was always so mean to the dog and that he ran away because of the awful sound of irritated wasps. "I think that this hedgehog was an angel," Mom said. She always compared everything to angels. "A sting angel", she added. "A sting angel?" Tanner asked in an astonished way. "Yeah, sure," she replied. "Why?" Tanner wanted to know.

"Well, that's obvious," - she suddenly became serious. - "Because he also showed you how you can protect yourself!"

That Tanner understood. "Yes, sometimes you need to do that by yourself, that's right," he admitted. For a moment he thought of his

Dad and his sister Katha who were gone, and whose grave had never been visited since the day of the funeral. The courage had failed him since then. No one had been able to get him to stand before this grave. Dad and his older sister Katha had died in an accident. Since then Tanner had never felt safe again.

Katha had often shown him flowers in the meadow and Dad had carried him on his shoulders or he told him the names of the stars in the sky.

Tanner remembered Katha's brown hair and her laugh. He still knew that he had felt safe when she was there, or Dad.

The best time was when Mom, Dad, Katha and he all sat together on the porch or if he and Katha looked for flowers.

But like a moody butterfly Katha had stolen herself away and never again he would find her or Dad. At least that was to be feared, and her grave would do nothing more than to support exactly this fact.

Life sometimes seemed very dangerous to him. Dangerous and empty.

In such moments he mostly liked to be alone and just by himself. Someone to talk to was just a burden then.

But now, after he met Sting, it felt differently.

Tanner smiled at Mom.

She smiled back and put a bottle filled with food on the table. "For Sting". She gave Tanner a small bowl into his hand. Tanner opened the bottle and went to the terrace, filling up the small bowl for the hedgehog.

That night he did not see Sting. Neither the following evenings. But he put a bowl of food every night at the place where he had met Sting first. Tanner knew that he owed it to his encounter with Sting that he now felt much less fear. And although Tanner did not see him again, he felt that Sting could not be far away. He felt exactly that Sting was around, maybe because of one thing:
Every morning the dish with the food was empty.

The next few months brought something very new: Kai, a boy from school who used to make fun of him had become something like his friend. The reason was probably the fact that Tanner helped his old cat and therefore Kai changed the way he was before.

He started becoming a real friend, though.

Just the other day he had give an old-fashioned receiver to Tanner, a special radio, for his tree house. Somehow today everything really fitted together so that he almost even looked for-ward to be going to school.

Just because he would spend time with Kai there. A shrill whistle brought him out of his thoughts: "Hey, Tanner! " It was Kai.

He grinned with a huge gap between his front teeth towards his direction. Tanner was just glad to see him.
Together they went their way through the forest towards school.
Mrs. Maida, the teacher, was pregnant, so that Tanner's class was taught together with the parallel class by Ms. Kirchberger, the substitute teacher, who kind of didn´t seem to like Tanner. Why that was like that, no one really knew.

But Tanner was convinced about one thing – that he had had to make twice the effort with her just to keep out of trouble.
This week he had to give a presentation to the class about animals in winter. Still on the way to school, he practiced with Kai. Tanner knew that Mrs. Kirchberger was not to be trifled with. The woodsman, before whom he was afraid, was even almost as bad as her.

But not quite as bad. From him came the sound of irritated wasps.

So you could understand something at least. But of Ms. Kirchberger there was no sound coming from. Not a single sound. That was much worse. An angry peace that might break at any moment to be accompanied by something threatful.

So it just happened to turn out today: Tanner was just about to report on the subject:

"Animals in winter". He had just listed precisely which birds flew to the south, and which birds remained in colder climates.

He started to name the raven birds when Angelina from the middle row announced that raven birds were terrible animals, because they would bring only misfortune into the world. Poor parents they are as well, remarked Ms. Kirchberger and added that the term "to be a raven parent" should be a really suitable insult for parents who neglected their kids.

Tanner could not believe how stupid his own teacher appeared, -even if it was only the substitute teacher. The fact that Angelina had talked like that wasn´t so much of a surprise, though. She knew no better. And with a teacher like Ms. Kirchberger it was probably also not quite guaranteed that children would learn anything decent.

"That's not true! " He shouted out those words more sharply than he had intended, but he didn´t care. Instead he went ahead. "this is nothing but dumb prejudice and totally stupid superstition! " Tanner was really outraged.

"How can you know that? " Ms. Kirchberger looked at him with all the derogatory condescension of which she was capable.

Most children would have been silenced by her eyes and the biting irony in her words alone. Tanner no longer recognized himself.

Upright and brave he stood in front of the class.

With his head held high he looked Ms. Kirchberger straight in the eyes: "I know it, because in my woods are a lot of ravens, and I have known them as long as I can remember. "

He thought of Kieran, the tame raven, and also he thought of the dead little raven, Ruby, who had died last spring.

He remembered how all the ravens of the forest had been placed around the poor, dead Ruby, crowded on the trees , and how their croaking had accompanied her death in a vast dirge. "They really are very social animals," he added, ‴"unlike you, Ms. Kirchberger."

The final part, he thought to himself only.

Tanner had decided that it would be going too far, so he held back what he actually wanted to say. Already, Tanner had already gone much too far for Ms. Kirchbergers terms.

"Your woods? "She asked mockingly. „Then this is probably your classroom as well? "

Some children laughed, among them Angelina. Others were silent, and looked as if they´d felt uncomfortable.

"Well," she added, „So here to avoid any mis-understanding I 'm going to ask the class to mark your paper. "

With an expression that should probably pretend concentration she looked around the room, and then she pointed the finger to Angelina.

„You there, Angelina, how did you like the presentation by Tanner? "

Angelina replied that she did not like it and that one shouldn´t rate it better than an F.

Ms. Kirchberger smiled contentedly and was carrying something in her teacher´s book.

„Nonsense!" Kai screamed suddenly in bet-ween. "Tanner really has named all the birds, he brought pictures, and he told everything in an informative and good way! "

After taking a short break in order to try to calm down he resumed:

"That was really great, Tanner even earned the best score, an A!" Kai still was full of excitement all red in the face." Calm down quickly," hissed Ms. Kirchberger threatening."

You're probably not going to believe seriously that your opinion is the one that will count here. " "Why not?" Kai wanted to know plenty befuddled. "That's probably obvious!"

His voice was as sweet as sugar and mischiefvous at the same time.

"Because you're his friend, of course! " Do you really believe because seriously, that I'll accept votes of friends?" She shook her head in mock despair, and then move into an indignant snort. "That would be nice. Wouldn´t it! "Ms. Kirchberger sank down on her teacher's chair and decided to reply then:

„Besides, I have not called you, and if you also believe that this is your classroom here, then you're just as crazy as this one there.

"She nodded her chin into Tanner' direction.

"But ...." Kai stammered desperately, Tanner waved his hand. He did not want Kai to be brought even further into trouble.

It was an unequal and a hopeless fight. "So to me it was also a good report!"

The resolute voice from the front row belonged to Jana, a girl who had Tanner been noticing more often.

She wore glasses with a pink frame, and her eyes were brown with little warm green spots in them. "Like everything and everyone," Ms. Kirchberger yawned. "That's not true ...." Jana tried to explain why she especially liked what Tanner had said, but Ms. Kirchberger would not let her go ahead.

Tanner took a guess at whom or what Jana did not like, namely Mrs. Kirchberger came into his mind. "You children make me sick," she scolded out of a sudden. "Every time I get home after school I need at least a brandy!"

That didn´t sound so good. Tanner did not believe that this could be normal.

Despite everything Tanner was proud of himself. At least a good start it had been.

Returned home, he told Mom about how stupid the teacher had been because of the ravens. "Tanner," Mom replied sternly, "to say that your teacher is stupid is not acceptable! Take that back, will you!" Tanner did not answer that, but instead told her about the liquor, that Ms. Kirchberger would have to drink right after school.

"Maybe Ms. Kirchberger should just do something else but teaching" suggested Mom, when he told her about it.

"Or maybe sometimes you just need a break from things ", she added. Of course, it was not possible that Ms. Kirchberger could have had heard this conversation.

Not even the cat was near when he and Mom had discussed that.

All the more it left Tanner stunned when she actually was missing the next day.

But, who knows. She was, after all, a teacher. For that- she probably couldn't be that stupid. She might have found out all by herself that she would need a break.

While Tanner was still wondering whether she would now, instead of teaching, perhaps be herding sheep for a while or maybe be intending to produce clay pots in a distant, warm country, Mrs. Schoenfelder, the director came in. Tanner has always liked her, and when she announced that she would take over the class in the next few weeks, he was glad.

Mrs. Schoenfelder was kind and friendly with the inner beauty of a deer, standing in the middle of the forest. A wonderful and gentle deer. "Would you present your paper again today, Tanner?"
She asked very gently. "Unfortunately I had no opportunity to prepare for the lessons." Tanner nodded. "Today," Tanner began, "I should like to come to the raven-birds".
He took his pen out of his pocket and held it up. Thus, began his lecture.

With last spring, with Kieran, the raven, and the fact that ravens were all wonderful friends and good parents anyway.

He told of Ruby, the little injured raven, which he had buried and he told of Kieran, who had comforted him then, and who had spent the night after Ruby's death with him in the tree house.

He also told of all the ravens, which had come to complain about Ruby's death, describing exactly how much they had taken to heart of the death of the little bird. "Raven parents are good parents," Tanner concluded.

This time, the lecture was a great success and normally that would also be sufficient to forget Ms. Kirchberger once and for all. But that did not work with Tanner.

The next day Tanner was not happy at all when he was told at breakfast, that Sam, the son of Mom's friend Renée, would come for a few weeks to live with them. Sam was only five, and that was no challenge for someone who was already nearly 13 years old like Tanner. But that was not all news. Mom tried to explain. She wanted to avoid the word "disabled" quite clearly, so she said something about "sun-childs" and about Down syndrome, and that Sam would see the world just differently to people without this particular trisomy, which was the medical name, but that would not be a reason to laugh at him.

Tanner hardly understood what she meant. To be laughed at - that was something he knew well, therefore he would never have thought of laughing at anyone - that was for sure.

Mom should know him well enough yet.

"Really?" - He said this intentionally stretched-out so that she should realize that there were simply things one did not need to tell him, Tanner.

Mom chewed, clearly relieved that she had now no justification for explaining anything. With a full mouth she avoided speaking, and so she chewed and munched, while Tanner thought about where Sam could sleep.

Suddenly it seemed quite appropriate to suggest that Sam could stay with him, in his room. Mom stopped chewing. She was happy, that was obvious. "Yes, great idea, indeed", she said, exceptionally with her mouth full, and her eyes lit up. After all, Sam could have slept on the sofa, but Tanner could not have shown him Gerda, the owl then.

He just had that idea that Gerda could help Sam in case he got homesick.

After all Sam was only five, and staying for a few weeks with people he did not know. Tanner was not so sure if Sam would handle that well. Therefore, he found that it could help to show Gerda to Sam. The lovely owl with her nocturnal flights around the house.

When Sam finally arrived, Tanner had to think about Moms first description of Sam. "Sun Child," she had said. And that really seemed to fit quite well. Sam actually looked like a laughing little sun. Even as his mother drove away again he beamed ahead and tried to catch the cat in order to stroke her a little.

He managed to touch her cat's tail only once, but then she was already gone.
"He's going to love Gerda," Tanner thought. His joy grew with the evening. He could hardly wait for it.
When Sam finally came out of the bathroom, and Tanner wanted to get comfortable on the mattress next to the bed Sam's mood changed

suddenly. Desperately he called for his mother, and neither he nor Mom knew what to do.
Fortunately, the cat appeared. This time she was more gracious than she had been in the morning.
Sam, who was quieter in her presence watched her with great interest. The cat approached his small, round face, and carefully nibbed his nose.
Immediately his face twitched again to a smile, only a little suspicious, then radiant again. "Sweet cat", he whispered, delighted.

Mama breathed a sigh of relief. "Well, then sleep tight." She pulled the door and while leaving she told her little guest: "Sam, if you need anything - just call me, or Tanner, ok?" Sam did not care about what she said.

Fascinated, he looked at the cat, which had now rolled up at the foot of the bed.

Apparently her decision to stay overnight with Tanner and Sam was fixed, and Tanner did not even intend to dissuade her from doing so. It only took a few minutes and Sam slept as deep as the cat. For a moment he wondered if he should wake him up again. Gerda would soon fly close by the house.

But when he saw him sleeping peacefully he decided not to wake him up. Instead he crept to the window from where he looked at her nightly flight undisturbed. He would surprise Sam the next day, Tanner thought, but suddenly Sam was awake again and looked with him with eyes wide open. "Hey, Sam. I'll show you something very nice!" Tanner promised him immediately. Sam laughed all over his face. "I'll show you an owl "" A ... an OWL?" Sam began to cry. "Shut down the blinds, please!"

He shivered all over again. Too puzzled, Tanner had the blind shut down automatically.
The evening light now only penetrated through a few tiny slits in the roller shutter.
"Close it, shut it", Sam whined.

"Now what if the owl is looking at me through the window sill?" He looked desperate.
Tanner wanted to help him.

After all, he was only five years old.

Tanner let the shutters shut down completely, so Sam could calm down. He began to roar- "It's dark", "make it bright" Sam sobbed.

Tanner quickly pressed the light switch. "Now it's bright again, Sam", he said, trying to remain calm. "Good," Sam said. "Thank you", now laying in the brightly lit room in the bed, the cat curled up at the foot end and slept in seconds. Still there were tears in his sleeping face, but he was breathing calmly. Also the next night Tanner had to close the shutter and put on the light. This time Sam did not sleep immediately. "Do you tell me a story?", He wanted to know from Tanner. So he told him about Mia, his friend, and that Mia was not afraid of anything at all. Of course it was a bit exaggerated, but Sam listened intently to him. "Is this Mia afraid of owls?" Tanner shook his head. "No, not at all!"."But when it's dark, Mia is afraid, right?" Tanner shook his head again. Sam looked quite impressed. "I used to be more frightened than I am today" said Tanner, so that Sam should not feel too weak. The little boy looked at him questioningly, and Tanner suddenly had an idea. Maybe he could show something to him. "Come on, we'll make shadow games on the wall!" He bent the lamp a little to the side so that the light could cast good shadows. Then he began to form shadow figures with his hands, which were enlarged on the wall. He showed Sam a shadow hare, a stork, an elephant and a cat. Sam liked the cat especially. "She's so big now", he said softly. "Look at this Sam", Tanner told him, "I do it all with my hands alone." You do not have to be afraid. This is not a big cat. It's just a shadow. The shadow of my hand. Do you see? This often looks much worse than it is."Sam nodded, but Tanner was not sure if he really understood. But then, out of a sudden he understood it himself. He understood it so well that he still knew it after Sam had left again, and it was confirmed by the fact that Sam has not had any more fear in the end while watching Gerda. After Sam had left, Tanner started to think about someone else again.

He still could not say why, but he couldn´t stop thinking about Ms.Kirchberger.

In the first few weeks it was o.k., but the longer she stayed away the more restless Tanner felt.

After a few weeks he could not stand it and cycled past her house.

Downstairs, at the entrance gate, were many names, not just hers. He hesitated a moment, then he pressed the bell with her name on it. A bright creaking got him a fright. There was the hum of the door opener.

She had simply pressed, just like that, without asking who exactly was there at all. Tanner wondered a little, but then he climbed up the stairs in the stairwell, so long until he came to an open door with Ms. Kirchberger standing in front of him and greeting him with a surprised face.

Actually, it was less of a greeting as it was a question: „What are you doing here?" she wanted to know. First without words, then she did ask this question. Tanner looked at her and thought about it. While he came up with no answer, it occurred to him that Ms. Kirchberger looked really sick. No wonder that she was still not back at school. Even after lots of hard thinking Tanner could not answer her question, because after all he did not know exactly what he was doing here. "I, Ummm ....", now that was embarrassing.

But even though he simply could not think of what to say at all, he already thought it was good that he was here now.

"Well, in this case - come in then, Tanner", said Mrs. Kirchberger, unfriendly as usual but with the light, hidden kindness in her eyes, she would have even denied with certainty.

At least she asked him to come into her apartment, he knew also that he would need to talk with Ms. Kirchberger. But about what? The door closed behind him.

Everywhere on the walls in the hallway were pictures of mountains, mountain peaks, but they resembled each other so much that he could hardly tell whether the images showed many different peaks or whether there was only one that had just been imaged from many different angles of view .

Ms. Kirchbergers shoes were neat and ordered by size.

The largest were walking shoes and stood in front. At the very far end stood elegant black evening shoes and somewhere in the middle Tanner saw the shoes again, which she had worn the entire school year while teaching.

Really a lot of shoes were there standing in that hallway - and many mountains where shown on the wall, too. Ms. Kirchberger had opened the door to the kitchen and asked quizzically, "Do you want to have a drink?"

Tanner nodded. He did not dare to utter a certain desire, even though he just realized that he would have preferred to drink a really hot cocoa. One with small pieces of chocolate in it, like Grandma always did it when she was a little nervous because of something or be-cause of nothing. He still felt a bit lost and suddenly out of place.

If only he had at least persuaded Kai to come along with him. Ms. Kirchberger left the door opened behind her, and Tanner watched as she poured mineral water into a glass while concentrating on some flowers in her room.

All of a sudden, as he watched her, Tanner got the idea that he was not the only one being, plagued by nervousness.

Slowly he followed her into the kitchen, took the glass, nodded his thanks to her without talking and then slipped onto the corner bench behind the table. Ms. Kirchberger stopped.
Almost frantically she began to polish the silverware next to the sink with a dish towel.
The kitchen clock ticked loudly and relentlessly into the silence. Ms. Kirchberger turned on the radio, and a deep, dark and friendly - sounding male voice filled the room. Up behind this man's voice now fought bravely Tanner 's voice itself up, and he heard himself say, "I wanted to know why you are the way you are ."

Well, now it was said. Ms. Kirchberger interrupted the circular motion, with which she had polished the cuterly and just asked,"Why. "

She looked completely stunned. "I do not know," Tanner replied.

That was the truth. He really did not know it.

Meanwhile, he looked at her. He knew that she had not treated him well, she wasn´t exactly like a teacher should be, and she knew that as well. Maybe he just wanted to find out why she had been so, so mean, well or just why she did what she did. Tanner really couldn´t say anything reasonable. The man's voice on the radio was still talking. Its pleasant sound helped across the long pauses during this bumpy, falter - the conversation.

Then finally Tanner just went out with it: "I wanted to know why you are so ... "

He started, after he had said this, because at the same moment the man's voice on the radio was silent, and a shallow piece of music whimpered softly all through the room.

Thunderstrucked Ms. Kirchberger looked at him. Tanner did not turn his eyes away anyway.

He looked at her - as if he would only accept the truth as an answer and nothing else. The empty, tired expression on Ms. Kirchberger's face changed.

That did not happen suddenly though, but was in a kind of slow motion like watching all sorts

of emotions on her face ; in various ways they showed up and again disappeared from it.
What remained was a single one: anger. "You want to know, why I am not a lovely, nice teacher, a teacher as they would probably appear in the wishful dreams of an average kindergarten child? "

With an intemperate movement she threw a spoon and a fork, which she had just been polishing to a high gloss onto the table.
Tanner nodded, a little frightened.

"Can´t you imagine? "Ms. Kirchberger wanted to know "that there once was a time in which I was just that perfect kind of teacher?"

Tanner did not dare to deny this question. First, it would probably appeared to be rude, on the other hand it dawned on him that behind this question has already been the hidden answer. Even if Tanner had intended to give her answer to this question – he couldn´t possibly imagine how. But the question was obviously the prelude to a speech surge, which uninhibitedly poured out of her.

"Yes, I once was like that, you can believe me," she ranted. "At that time I did not yet know what mean creatures kids can possibly turn into .

What had begun with a great anger in her voice abruptly ended in a miserable, frustrated sigh and a silence that now discharged all what had previously jammed inside her, trembling and surging like invisible waves which slowly became smaller and quieter.

Tanner thought of the nameless and numerous adults who had put him in such great fear before he met Sting.

Even if what Ms. Kirchberger just said sounded kind of odd: Tanner knew at once exactly what she was talking about. He understood that her huge fear of children must have been as great as his own fear concerning adults. And maybe she wasn't totally wrong. From his own experience he knew at least how mean kids could actually be.In this regard they differed not necessarily from adults.

Especially not if you did not know them as closely and if they weren't at a point yet where they would trust a person like Ms. Kirchberger.

Then an idea appeared in his mind. If Ms. Kirchberger could have also just such a friend as Sting, he thought, she would learn that most of the kids just sounded like little mice. Those little mice, he had to admit that after all, were able to place themselves in positions that made at least their shadows appear dangerous. But basically there were mice - in the best case hares. Sting, he was sure about that, would be just the right thing, the right friend for Ms. Kirchberger. She had, while Tanner was still lost in thoughts, sat down. It was obvious: she felt ashamed because of her emotional melt-down. That was not hard to read from her face. Tanner took a short breath, and then he told her everything of Sting, the magical hedgehog. He forgot nothing, and while he was telling her about him the color in Ms. Kirchbergers face returned.

Not only that, in addition to her color she also, out of a sudden appeared quite young and pretty.

As he looked at her he thought that this could be just the way she might have looked before she had become the current Ms. Kirchberger, the one with whom he had been so plagued by. For a moment there was silence again.

The man's voice on the radio finally announced something about the reopening of a shopping center. And then Ms. Kirchberger began to tell something.

It was something of an old philosopher from Greece, a story that was called "The Allegory of the Cave" by some wise man.

There was a saying that people were trapped in a dark cave so that they could see no other people and nothing of life outside. They could only see the shadows and they thought that the shadows would be the real world.

There was something true in it. Sometimes it had felt a little weird to hear these animal-sounds. The sounds which stood for each person. But now, with the Allegory of the Cave" it somehow did fit together much better.

He had stepped a little out of the cave with the help of Sting, he just saw little more than the

shadow. Ms. Kirchberger also did see more, he could tell now clearly. And he heard it.
Satisfied, he drank the last of his water. "I must go now," he said at last.

Ms. Kirchberger accompanied him to the door. His own footsteps echoed after him in the stairwell.

As he unlocked his bike, he looked again up to the window of her apartment.
There she stood and looked differently and kind of changed in some different little ways.
In ways, he could not describe.

He had not told her that he had heard what kind of animal she was: was a bird, namely a blackbird.

And certainly there was behind its shadow much, much more. Just as like it is in the shade.

As he drove away from her so he knew it had been a good idea to visit her.

More fear had left him and he felt so entirely fearless at that very moment.

He could not explain that, but suddenly he took the road that lead to the cemetery. By bike it was not even that far.

The grave he would have found himself with his eyes closed. It was located directly behind the first course of the main entrance, directly under a pine tree. But it never came into question today, on this day to close the eyes.

Their names were written on the grave stone and yet he knew suddenly that this grave stone was only a shadow. A monument.

Nothing more. The grave was decorated very beautifully and there was a candle burning as well. Mom had probably been there lately. Whether she knew what was now clear to him?

Neither Dad nor Katha were here. It was just a place that should remind of them.

It was nothing more than a shadow of what Papa and Katha used to be.
And suddenly he knew that he had really heard some time ago in the forest. They had been there with him.

They were never far away. Although they were no longer visible because they had gone out of the shadows and no one, who still was caught in the shadow could see what ever there was above.

But in the midst of his forest, his wonderful forest to which he returned in the evening, he got an idea, a slight idea of what awaited him beyond the shadow - and who.

Someday in the future. When the forest would have changed his appearance for many, many times.

The first one he saw in his forest from afar was Horst, the tame wild boar.

Horst was curious, as always, but Tanner did not want to talk about Ms. Kirchberger and he didn´t feel like talking to him about the cemetry.

Horst looked after him with a quite sly look interested and inquisitive as usual, but Tanner did not give in.

Horst really did not need to know everything. Especially not these things.

Because he would save that for Sting, for Mom, maybe for Kai, or for his friend Mia who would come to visit him over the holidays.

He would simply not tell it to anyone who came running up like Horst. He wouldn´t share it with someone as curious and as impatient for that story was too important to him.

For this story it took time. It took a lot of time, and also a little rest.

It was a story for friends.

For real friends and for those who were most important, that was for sure.

Vocabulary
(German book by Claudia J. Schulze available too)

1affectionate anhänglich, liebevoll

2allegory Allegorie, Gleichnis

3 appearance Erscheinung

4 average durchschnittlich

5 blackbird Amsel

6 boar Wildschwein

7 brave tapfer

8 candle Kerze

9 capable (to be capable) fähig sein

10 cave Höhle

11 choppy abgehackt

12 condescension Herablassung

13 creatures Kreaturen

14 curious neugierig

15 cemetry Friedhof

16 deer Wild (z.B. Hirsch)

17 (to) echo hallen, schallen

18 frantically hektisch

19 frustrated frustriert

20 (to) fit passen

21 frightened ängstlich

22 footsteps Schritte

23 hedgehog Igel

We support these organisations:

http://www.wegweiser-hospiz-palliativmedizin.de/angebot/1258-kinderhospiz_sterntaler

http://www.tannheim.de/index.php/spenden.html

http://www.palliativzentrum-vs.de/

Please feel free to donate something if you like. Thank you.

Contact: CJ.Schulze@gmx.de
Text: Claudia J. Schulze
Revised by Tim Holden, illustrated by Anke Hartmann

Tanner and the little raven

Claudia J. Schulze / Tim Holden/ Anke Hartmann